T
S

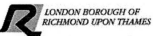

C...TIONS

IZZI HOWELL

Franklin Watts

First published in Great Britain in 2019 by
The Watts Publishing Group

Copyright © The Watts Publishing Group, 2019

Produced for Watts by
White-Thomson Publishing Ltd
www.wtpub.co.uk

Series Editor: Izzi Howell
Consultant: Philip Parker
Series Designer: Rocket Design (East Anglia) Ltd
Designer: Clare Nicholas

ISBN: 978 1 4451 6121 1 (HB) 978 1 4451 6122 8 (PB)
10 9 8 7 6 5 4 3 2 1

Franklin Watts
An imprint of
Hachette Children's Group
Part of The Watts Publishing Group
Carmelite House
50 Victoria Embankment
London EC4Y 0DZ

An Hachette UK Company
www.hachette.co.uk

www.franklinwatts.co.uk

Printed in China

Picture acknowledgements:
Alamy: North Wind Picture Archives 7b, De Luan 11t, Granger Historical Picture Archive 11b, Universal Images Group
North America LLC 15, Heritage Image Partnership Ltd 19b, Greek photonews 23b; Getty: Richmatts cover and 17b,
argalis 8, dimitris_k 10 and 30, ilbusca 17t, ZU_09 19t, VCG Wilson/Corbis 20b, Encyclopaedia Britannica/UIG 23t,
imagestock 25t; Metropolitan Museum: The Bothmer Purchase Fund, 1978 5t, Fletcher Fund, 1938 13t, Fletcher Fund,
1931 3t and 20t, Rogers Fund, 1911 21, Rogers Fund, 1913 27t, Rogers Fund, 1916 29t; Shutterstock: Samot 5b, vivooo 6,
Josep Curto 7t, Kamira 9t, Peter Hermes Furian 9b, Patalakha Sergii 12, Panos Karas 13b, Vdant85 14t, Marius G 14b,
RossHelen 16, baldovina 18, EDUARDO AUSTREGESILO 22, Lefteris Papaulakis 3b , 24 and 27b, brulove 25bl, ulrich22
25bc, Kovaleva_Ka 25br, Alfio Ferlito 26, Aerial-motion 28, ANCH 29b and 31.

All design elements from Shutterstock.

CONTENTS

THE ANCIENT GREEKS

Who?

The first great Greek civilisations were the Minoans, who lived on the island of Crete from 3000 to 1450 BCE, and the Mycenaeans, who lived on mainland Greece from 1650 to 1100 BCE. After the Mycenaeans, Greece entered a three-hundred-year period known as the Dark Ages. The Greeks of the Dark Ages stopped writing, creating detailed artworks and building large settlements.

Bulls were very important in Minoan culture. This stone carving was found in a palace in Knossos, Crete.

Around 800 BCE, small villages began to grow into cities. Each city became a separate city-state, controlled by its own ruler. This is partly because Greece's geography of islands and mountains physically separated different areas, so they developed independently. During this time, known as the Archaic period, a more advanced civilisation started to return to Greece.

This map shows some of the important places and city-states in ancient Greece. There were over 1,000 city-states across the Greek world.

The height of the ancient Greek civilisation was the Classical period, which lasted from 508 to 323 BCE. This was a time of scientific discoveries, new ideas about philosophy and theatre, and the beginnings of democracy. During the Hellenistic period (323 to 30 BCE), the ancient Greeks controlled a huge territory across the Mediterranean and the Middle East.

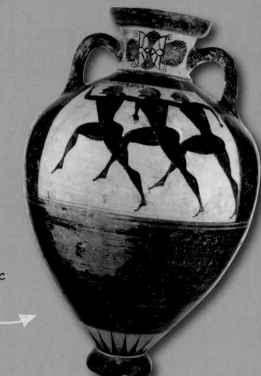

This jar was given as a prize during the Panathenaic Games, in which different city-states competed against each other (see pages 28–29).

What happened?

From the second and first centuries BCE onwards, the Romans and other groups started to take control of Greece and other areas that had been Greek territory. The civilisations that took over the Greek world were influenced by many aspects of ancient Greek culture. The legacy of ancient Greek civilisation lives on today in modern politics, architecture and language.

The remains of this temple can be seen in Delphi, Greece. There are ruins of many ancient Greek buildings across Europe and the Middle East.

CITY-STATES

Ancient Greece was not one country politically. It was divided up into small city-states, such as Athens, Sparta and Corinth. Although people across Greece spoke the same language and followed the same religion, people considered themselves Athenians or Spartans, rather than Greeks.

GENIUS ★ ★
ORGANISED COMMUNITIES

Local identities

Many different social groups lived in each city-state, including citizens (born in the city-state), slaves and non-citizens. These social groups were united by a shared city-state identity. Everyone in a city-state came together to celebrate unique festivals, and gathered in specially built places, such as the *agora* (meeting place).

The agora in Athens sat at the foot of the Acropolis (raised area). The remains of the agora are open to visitors today.

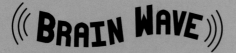

These coins from Athens are decorated with the goddess Athena, the patron of the city, and an owl, a symbol of Athena.

Different rulers

City-states were ruled in different ways, such as monarchies (rule of a king/queen) or oligarchies (rule of a few leading people). Eventually, one city-state developed a style of ruling that worked particularly well. In 508, the city-state of Athens became a democracy (rule of the people). Men who were born in Athens could vote on how the city-state was run (see pages 10-11).

At war

City-states fought each other to show power and to gain new territory. The most famous war between city-states was the Peloponnesian War between Athens and Sparta (431 to 404 BCE). Almost every Greek city-state joined in the war, fighting as allies of one of the two sides. City-states also worked together to fight a common enemy, such as the Persian Empire.

In the fifth century, allied city-states, including Athens, Corinth and Megara, came together to fight against the Persian Empire, which was trying to conquer Greek territory.

THE GREEK WORLD

Around the middle of the eighth century BCE, ancient Greek city-states started to set up new colonies abroad. They chose areas with fertile lands for farming and access to various natural resources.

GENIUS
★ ★
NEW TERRITORY

Exchanging ideas

City-states set up colonies around the Mediterranean Sea and across Europe, in areas known today as Sicily, Italy, France, Spain and North Africa. Settlers spread ancient Greek culture and customs to these new territories. They also learned from and were influenced by the people already living in these areas.

Settlers introduced typical Greek buildings to their colonies, such as this theatre (see pages 26–27) in Syracuse, Italy.

TEST of TIME

Many modern cities started out as new settlements in Greek colonies. For example, settlers from the Greek island of Rhodes established the port of Neapolis in Italy, which is now the city of Naples. The colony of Massilia, begun by settlers from a Greek city-state in Turkey, is now the French city of Marseille.

Alexander's empire

Alexander the Great was the king of the city-state of Macedonia (see page 4). He went beyond the few colonies established by other city-states and in 334 BCE started conquering huge areas of territory across Egypt, Syria, Iraq, Turkey and even as far east as India. Eventually, he controlled an empire of over 5 million square km.

This marble head of Alexander the Great was once attached to the body of a full statue.

WOW!

Alexander the Great never lost a single battle!

A new age

Alexander the Great's giant empire marked the beginning of the age of Hellenistic Greece. The ancient Greek language and customs spread across the Mediterranean and Middle East, and mixed with the culture of newly conquered areas. For example, in Egypt, the new Greek rulers called themselves pharaohs to please the ancient Egyptian people.

This map shows Alexander's empire at its greatest size in 323 BCE.

DEMOCRACY

During the Classical period (508 to 323 BCE), the city-state of Athens developed a new form of government called democracy – rule of the *demos* (people). Most governments around the world today are democracies.

GENIUS ★ PEOPLE POWER

Male voters

Even though democracy meant rule by the people, only male citizens of Athens (those born in the city) could vote. Women, slaves or people from other city-states were not allowed to take part. Male voters could attend assembly meetings almost weekly to choose new leaders and decide how to punish crimes or whether to go to war. They voted with a show of hands — the majority won the vote. This is unlike modern democracy, in which people elect representatives to make these decisions on their behalf.

Assembly meetings took place on Pnyx Hill in Athens. Voters sat on the hill (seen in the foreground of this photograph) and listened to speakers.

Keeping things fair

A council of 500 men, known as the Boule, was in charge of running the city-state. Members of the Boule were chosen randomly by drawing lots. They were only allowed to serve for one year, and never more than twice in their lifetime. This was considered the fairest way to have an even selection of men from across the city-state. Holding elections would have given well-known or wealthy men an advantage.

The members of the Boule attended meetings almost every day.

(((BRAIN WAVE)))

Voters could vote to banish dangerous leaders who were too ambitious or power-crazy. To do this, men carved the name of the politician on a shard of pottery called an ostrakon. If enough people voted, the leader could be exiled from the city for ten years. *Ostrakon* is the root of the modern word 'ostracise', which means to exclude.

WARFARE

Organisation was an important factor in the success of Greek armies. Soldiers were well trained and knew how to work and move together on the battlefield.

GENIUS ★ ORGANISED SOLDIERS

Hoplites

The ancient Greek army was mainly made up of foot soldiers called hoplites. They fought in organised groups called phalanxes. In a phalanx, hoplites stood in close rows with their round shields locked together for protection. The first rows held their spears horizontally to stop the enemy from getting close. When the phalanx marched together, it was very hard for the enemy to break through their ranks.

TEST OF TIME

The word phalanx is still used today to describe a group of people standing or moving closely together.

Hoplites in a phalanx formation. Each hoplite provided his own equipment, which included a shield, a spear, a metal helmet and armour.

Training soldiers

The city-state of Sparta was famous for its military training. Boys left their families and trained as soldiers from the age of seven. During training, soldiers weren't given enough food to eat or warm clothes to wear, as it was believed that this made them tough. The training seemed to work, as Spartan soldiers were famous for their fierce fighting spirit.

WOW!

In one battle, reports say that Spartan soldiers fought with their hands and teeth after losing their swords!

Ancient Greek soldiers fought with metal-tipped spears. They used a short sword for close combat.

Working out weaknesses

Alexander the Great (see page 9) was well known for his excellent battle tactics. He identified his enemies' weaknesses and organised his troops to attack them where they were vulnerable. This helped him to beat armies that were much larger than his own.

This modern statue of Alexander the Great riding his horse Bucephalus stands in the city of Thessaloniki, Greece. Soldiers on horseback became an important part of ancient Greek armies from the fifth century BCE.

(((BRAIN WAVE)))

One of Alexander's best tactical victories was at the Battle of Gaugamela in 331 BCE. Alexander beat the Persian king Darius III, even though Darius had a larger army and chose the fighting ground to his advantage. Alexander won by drawing the sides of the enemy's army into battle so that the middle (where Darius was) was left exposed. In the end, the Persian army retreated.

SHIPS

The ancient Greeks used ships for trade and transport. They were also important weapons, used to defend Greek territory against invasion.

GENIUS ★ SMASHING SHIPS

Smooth sailing

Ships were an obvious choice to transport cargo between Greece's many islands and territory outside the mainland. Sailing was often easier than travelling across land, as much of Greece is rocky and mountainous. Ships used for trading were powered by sails.

Trading ships sailed close to shore so as not to get lost.

(((BRAIN WAVE)))

At Corinth, there is a narrow land bridge that links the north and south parts of Greece. Ships had to sail all the way around the south of Greece to get from one side to the other, which took a long time. To solve this problem, the ancient Greeks built the Diolkos – a stone track over the narrow piece of land. The ships' cargo and even the ships themselves could be pulled across the track to the other side. Today there is a canal for ships.

Rowing into battle

Ancient Greek warships were called triremes. They were very lightweight, with three rows of oars on each side. The oars overlapped at different levels so as not to waste space. In battle, sailors rowed the triremes at superfast speeds, and could easily move the ship in the direction they wanted to travel.

The overlapping oars of a trireme were below deck, which kept the top deck clear for fighting. After an enemy ship was rammed, enemy sailors often jumped onto the trireme to continue the battle.

Crash!

The ancient Greeks didn't have effective weapons that could be used to attack other ships from a distance. Instead, they rowed their trireme right up to an enemy ship and crashed into it with the bronze tip of the boat, which acted as a ram. This made a hole in the enemy ship, breaking it apart or sinking it.

ARCHITECTURE

Ancient Greek architecture was simple yet sophisticated. Architects followed sets of rules when designing buildings, which meant that many buildings were built in a similar style.

GENIUS ★ DESIGN ★ ORDERED

Shape and material

Nearly all Greek buildings were rectangular, with columns inside to support the roof. The first buildings were made of wood. Later, marble and limestone were used for many grand public buildings. Both of these stones are easily found across Greece.

TEST of TIME

Ancient Greek architecture has inspired many architects throughout history, from Roman times up until the present day. You can see Greek-inspired buildings in most modern cities.

At the remains of the Temple of Zeus in Olympia, the beams that supported the roof can still be seen at the top of the columns.

Different styles

Balance, order and symmetry were very important to Greek architects. They developed three different styles of architecture, called Doric, Ionic and Corinthian. Most ancient Greek buildings were built in one of these three styles. For this reason, many buildings look alike.

The differences between Doric, Ionic and Corinthian buildings are most obvious in the style of their columns.

scrolled top

Ionic

ornately decorated top with leaves and scrolls

24 sides

plain top

Corinthian

20 sides

24 sides

large base

Doric

no base

small base

Seen from afar

Grand ancient Greek buildings, such as temples, were designed to be admired from far away. Architects learned tricks to make these large buildings look more visually appealing from a distance. They made columns slightly thicker at the bottom and positioned them to lean slightly inwards. The corner columns were also made slightly larger. When seen from far away, this creates an optical illusion that every line of the building is perfectly straight.

The Parthenon temple was built on the Acropolis (see page 6) in the centre of Athens, so that it could be seen from across the city.

WRITING

The legacy of ancient Greek writing lives on today through its alphabet. Written records of Greek ideas about science, mathematics and philosophy have influenced many great thinkers.

A new alphabet

The ancient Greek alphabet developed around 800 BCE. It was based on the Phoenician alphabet, but the Greeks added new letters representing vowels. This allowed them to write words that more closely represent the sounds of spoken words. The Greek alphabet was passed on to other groups, including the Romans, and is still used in Greece today.

There are many examples of ancient Greek text carved into stone, such as this law code engraved on a public building in Gortyn, Crete. Every other line of the text is written backwards, which was a common style of public writing.

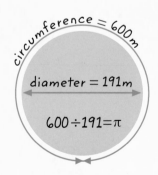

TEST OF TIME

Today, Greek letters are used as symbols in maths and science. The symbol for the greek letter *pi* (π) is used to represent the number 3.142, which is the result of a circle's circumference divided by its diameter.

circumference = 600m

diameter = 191m

$600 \div 191 = \pi$

Types of text

Many Greek texts survive to this day, including accounts of historical events and exploration, and books about philosophy, science, medicine, astronomy and maths. We can also read ancient Greek epic stories, such as the *Iliad* and the *Odyssey*. These stories tell the tale of the Trojan War and the journey home of the hero Odysseus. They are fictional, but may have been partly based on real events.

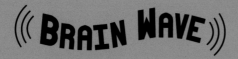

((BRAIN WAVE))

Before the Greek Classical period, most accounts of history were a mixture of fact and fiction, combining elements from myths and real events. Greek historians, such as Herodotus, took a new approach and started to record events as accurately as possible. This inspired later historians to do the same.

In the *Odyssey*, Odysseus has to escape from a cyclops — a mythical one-eyed giant.

The Alexandria library

In the city of Alexandria, in Greek-controlled Egypt, was one of the largest libraries in the ancient world. The library contained Greek books and foreign texts, so visitors had access to many new ideas and observations in one place. Later the library burned down and the texts were lost forever. It is only because of Arabic translations of these ancient texts, which were later translated into other languages, that we know about them today.

This nineteenth-century drawing suggests what it would have been like inside the Library of Alexandria. Visitors are reading from the library's collection of papyrus scrolls.

ART

Right from the beginning of the ancient Greek civilisation, the human body was the inspiration for their art. They developed different ways to represent the body in art, of which mainly sculpture and pottery survive today.

Different bodies

The ancient Greeks wanted the human body to look as lifelike as possible in their art. They showed people doing a range of activities and in many different poses. The human body was often shown naked, as the Greeks believed this showed the model as a hero.

This vase is painted with images of women weaving. Historians look at art to learn about everyday life and activities in ancient Greece.

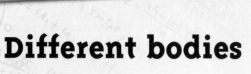

Painting pottery

The ancient Greeks used plain pottery pots to store and transport liquids, such as wine or oil. They also produced elaborately painted pottery as pieces of art. Ancient Greek pottery was usually painted in just a few different colours. This made the designs stand out. Painters used delicate, precise lines to show the details. They often added geometric patterns for decoration.

This Minoan pot is decorated with an intricate painting of an octopus.

Skilled sculptors

Highly skilled ancient Greek sculptors used tiny chisels to carve delicate details that brought their sculptures to life. Every detail in the human body was recreated in stone.

This ancient Greek sculpture is full of details, from the creases in the skin on the hands to the subtle folds in clothing.

WOW!

Ancient Greek sculptures were originally painted in bright colours! They look plain today because the paint has worn away over time.

TEST of TIME

During the European Renaissance in the fourteenth to seventeenth centuries, artists such as Michelangelo were inspired by ancient Greek art. They captured the details of the human body, and made their artworks full of movement.

ASTRONOMY

Many ancient civilisations, such as the Egyptians and Babylonians, used the movements of the Sun and the planets to keep track of time. However, the ancient Greeks wanted to take it a step further and understand what they saw in the stars and why.

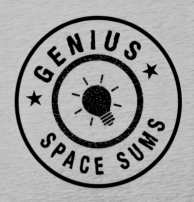

During lunar eclipses, ancient Greek astronomers saw the circular shadow of the Earth projected on to the Moon, which confirmed their theory of a round Earth.

Observation and explanation

The ancient Greeks began by closely observing the sky and coming up with theories that explained what they saw. For example, based on their observation that ships disappear as they move towards the horizon, they correctly worked out that the Earth was round, and not flat as some believed. They also noticed that stars appear to move higher in the sky as you move towards the south, which suggests that the Earth is curved.

Geometry

Astronomers used geometry (the maths of shapes) to work out the dimensions of the Earth. The astronomer Eratosthenes calculated the Earth's circumference by measuring the angle of the Sun in the sky in two different Egyptian cities. The Sun was directly above one city at noon, but not quite as high in another at the same time. He then measured the distance between the two cities and used these figures to work out the circumference. He was not exactly correct, but very close!

Eratosthenes worked out that the circumference of the Earth was about fifty times the distance between the two cities.

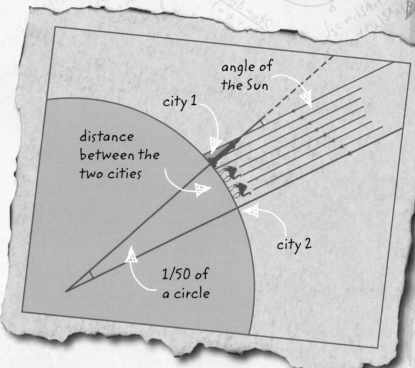

angle of the Sun

city 1

distance between the two cities

city 2

1/50 of a circle

New instruments

Ancient Greek astronomers developed new tools to help them with their research. The astrolabe was an instrument that measured the angles of objects in space in relation to each other, which helped astronomers to work out their movements. The Antikythera mechanism was a clockwork machine made of bronze that calculated the positions of the stars and the Sun and predicted eclipses.

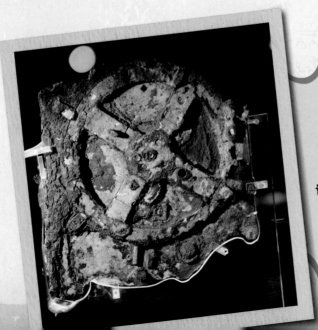

The remains of the Antikythera mechanism were found in a shipwreck off the coast of the Greek island Antikythera in 1902.

WOW!

The Antikythera mechanism is considered to be the world's first analogue computer!

MEDICINE

Ancient Greek doctors used ideas taken from philosophy, such as looking for logical answers, to try to better understand the human body. Their ideas influenced medicine for thousands of years afterwards, and still do so today.

GENIUS ★ RATIONAL REMEDIES

Natural causes and cures

The early ancient Greeks believed that diseases were caused by bad luck and could be cured by praying or pleasing the gods. This changed when ancient Greek doctors began trying to understand how the human body works in order to find logical causes and cures for diseases.

Early ancient Greeks prayed to Asclepius, the god of medicine, to cure their diseases. His stick and snake are used as a symbol to represent medicine today.

WOW!

Ancient Greek doctors were some of the first to observe and try to treat conditions such as diabetes and intestinal worms!

In balance

The ancient Greek doctor Hippocrates put forward the theory that the human body contained four substances — blood, phlegm, yellow bile and black bile. He suggested that too much or too little of one substance caused illness. To cure illnesses, doctors tried to balance the substances, for example by bleeding a patient if they had 'too much blood'. Although this theory was not correct, it was an important early example of doctors trying to logically understand and treat disease.

Ancient Greek doctors examined patients and observed their symptoms to try to understand what was wrong.

To cure patients with too much phlegm, doctors gave them barley soup, vinegar and honey.

TEST of TIME

Modern doctors have to promise to keep patients' medical history a secret and to try their best to help them. This is known as the Hippocratic Oath and dates back to Hippocrates' ideas about how doctors should behave.

THEATRE

Ancient Greek plays were held in front of very large audiences. Special techniques were developed to help everyone follow what was happening on stage.

GENIUS
★ ★
AUDIENCE ACOUSTICS

Shape and space

Greek theatres were built in a semicircular shape with tiered seating, so that everyone could see what was happening on stage. Actors performed on a raised stage in the centre. In front of this stage was a flat area where members of the chorus performed. The chorus sang and danced, commenting on the events of the play.

The limestone seats at Epidauros also block low frequency background noise, such as talking in the audience.

(((BRAIN WAVE)))

The theatre at Epidauros has brilliant acoustics, which help the audience to hear the actors. The steps of limestone seats boost high-frequency sounds, such as the actors' voices. Historians aren't sure if this design was deliberate or accidental. However, it worked so well that the Greeks copied it in other theatres.

Comedies and tragedies

Greek plays were often comedies or tragedies. Comedies were funny and rude, with slapstick jokes and stereotypical characters. Tragedies were sad stories, which often presented a moral lesson about what is right or wrong. Playwrights wrote new plays for drama festivals, the very best of which were given prizes.

This pottery figure dating from ancient Greece represents a stereotypical old woman character from a Greek comedy. This type of character appeared in many Greek comedies.

WOW!

A wooden crane was sometimes used on stage to allow actors playing gods to fly through the air.

Masks

Greek actors often wore masks with exaggerated facial expressions. This helped faraway audience members to see how the characters were feeling. It also meant that actors could quickly and easily change roles without confusing the audience.

This is a stone model of a typical Greek mask. No original Greek masks survive today, as they were made from painted fabric that has decomposed. However, we know what the masks look like from models made in other materials.

SPORTS

There were at least four sport festivals in ancient Greece, the most famous of which was the Olympic Games at Olympia. The first games were held in 776 BCE as part of a religious festival. Over time, they became more political, as city-states sent representatives to compete away from the battlefield.

Calling a truce

One month before the games, a truce was called. Messengers travelled across the Greek world, spreading news of the upcoming games. Any wars or disputes between city-states were put on hold. The truce meant that athletes from different city-states could safely travel to and from Olympia, without fear of attack.

Events

The first Olympic Games lasted for just one day, with running races as the only events. Later, more events were added and the games were extended to last five days. These events included chariot and horse racing, wrestling, boxing and running.

Today, the remains of the running track at Olympia can still be seen. The shot put events at the 2004 Athens Olympics were held here.

TEST of TIME

The marathon – a 42.19-km race – is based on an ancient Greek myth of a messenger who ran around this distance to report the end of a war. However, it was not an event at the ancient Olympics and was only invented in 1896 for the modern Olympics.

WOW!

The most extreme event at the ancient Olympics was pankration — a violent mixture of wrestling and boxing. There were almost no rules, but competitors couldn't bite each other or poke each other's eyes out!

This vase shows a pankration match. In pankration, competitors could kick, hit and choke each other.

Gifts and glory

Athletes were motivated to take part in the games to bring glory to their city-state. Although winners only received a laurel wreath at the Olympics, they returned home to fame and fortune. Their names were recorded and news of their victory, and that of their city-state, spread across the Greek world.

laurel leaves

GLOSSARY

acoustics — how well sound can be heard in a place

ally — an area or country that has agreed to help another area, especially in a war

cargo — goods carried by a large vehicle, such as a ship

circumference — the length of the edge of a circle or curved shape

citizen — someone who lives in a certain area or city and has special rights because they were born there

city-state — a city and the area around it, ruled by one leader

colony — an area controlled by another country, often far away

conquer — to take control of an area by force

custom — a habit or tradition

decomposed — decayed and gradually destroyed

democracy — rule of the people. In Athenian democracy, male citizens of Athens could vote on how the city was run. In modern democracy, people vote for representatives who run the country on their behalf

exile — when someone is forced to leave their home and live somewhere else

hoplite — an ancient Greek foot soldier

monarchy — rule of a monarch (a king or queen from a royal family)

oligarchy — rule of a few rich or powerful people

phalanx — a group of hoplites who fought closely together

ram — a piece of equipment used to crash into something

settle — to start living in a place

settlement — a place where people live

stereotypical — having qualities that are expected of a certain type of person

tactics — the planning and organisation of soldiers in a war

territory — land controlled by a group of people

tiered — with several layers

truce — an agreement to stop fighting for a period of time

TIMELINE

3000 to 1450 BCE	The Minoan civilisation develops on the island of Crete.
1650 to 1100 BCE	The Mycenaean civilisation thrives on mainland Greece.
1100 to eighth century BCE	The Greek Dark Ages
eighth century to 508 BCE	The Archaic period
776 BCE	The first Olympic Games are held at Olympia.
508 to 323 BCE	The Classical period
508 BCE	The first democracy is set up in Athens.
431 to 404 BCE	The Peloponnesian War takes place between Athens and Sparta.
334 BCE	Alexander the Great starts to conquer territories as part of his empire.
323 BCE	Alexander the Great dies.
323 to 30 BCE	The Hellenistic period

INDEX

FURTHER INFORMATION

Websites

www.natgeokids.com/uk/discover/history/greece/
10-facts-about-the-ancient-greeks/

www.bbc.co.uk/guides/zxytpv4

www.dkfindout.com/uk/history/ancient-greece/

Books

Ancient Greece (Facts and Artefacts) by Tim Cooke (Franklin Watts, 2018)

Alexander the Great and the Ancient Greeks by David Gill (Franklin Watts, 2018)

Ancient Greece (Technology in the Ancient World) by Charlie Samuels (Franklin Watts, 2015)